The Tarot of Power

Joe Cavanaugh

symbiotic solutions

Copyright © 2011 by Joe Cavanaugh.

Library of Congress Cataloging-in-Publication Data is available.

ISBN 978-0-578-07619-5

10 9 8 7 6 5 4 3 2 1

The Major Arcana as a Source of Power

The power of the Symbols of the Tarot lies within its intrinsic nature to stimulate thought. By illuminating the past, clarifying the present, and envisioning possible futures, Symbols of the Tarot facilitate awareness, adaptability, and creativity. These abilities can be focused to create health, wealth, and power.

To help in your endeavors, my suggestion regarding Tarot spreads is to use as many and any of them as you like. Most likely, you will develop your own way of using the symbols based upon your intent. One spread that I've found useful is to lay out all of the images in numerical order 0–21. Then, I'll run an idea through each symbol to see if I've done everything possible to manifest my vision. The rigorous thought process stimulates creative action.

The essence of this book is to enable you to achieve goals. Create the reality you desire. Recognize and take advantage of patterns. Invigorate your passions and develop deep insight. Emerge victorious in your adventures.

Best of luck,
Joe

Tarot Symbols of the Major Arcana

0 **The Fool:** Impulse leads to action.
1 **The Wizard:** Use knowledge and willpower to produce effects.
2 **The Priestess:** Use intuition to help make good decisions.
3 **The Empress:** Create what you need.
4 **The Emperor:** Take advantage of opportunities through leadership.
5 **The Priest/Monk/Hierophant:** Develop habits that lead to success.
6 **The Lovers:** Develop symbiotic relationships.
7 **The Chariot:** Establish control and time your actions to achieve victory.
8 **Justice:** Understand cause and effect over time.
9 **The Hermit:** Develop insight.
10 **The Wheel of Fortune:** Adapt to changes in the environment.
11 **Strength/Lust:** Use passions as sources of energy, drive, and power.
12 **The Hanged Man:** Attain enlightenment regarding necessary metamorphosis.
13 **Death:** Solve problems, eliminate inaccurate perceptions, and end bad habits.
14 **Temperance/Art:** Create useful tools and manage resources.
15 **The Devil:** Balance temptation/concentration to successfully explore/achieve.
16 **The Tower:** Build strengths, consolidate gains, and progress to new frontiers.
17 **The Star:** Use guides to navigate and course correct when necessary.
18 **The Moon:** Develop accurate perceptions.
19 **The Sun:** Absorb energy for renewal, clarity, and growth.
20 **Judgment/Aeon/Angel:** Take necessary risks, engage in action, and judge progress.
21 **The World:** Develop wisdom and strength from experience.
0 **The Fool:** Your next impulse . . .

0 ✦ THE FOOL

Essence
Impulse leads to action

Question
Am I excited to learn and interact when venturing forth or am I dangerously reckless, with no regard for accumulating knowledge? Have I considered whether my impulse will lead me to treasure or ruin? Am I prepared?

Revelation
The symbol of The Fool represents an impulse that leads to action. Take action with all senses of perception fully engaged. Or, proceed unprepared, unwary, and unwilling to learn. The manner of travel will help to determine whether you succeed or fail.

By choosing to consider the collective wisdom of the ages inherent in each of the 21 Tarot Symbols of The Major Arcana, you will increase the probability of achieving your goals. The Tarot Symbols reveal the threads of continuity that exist in our ever-changing world.

Accrue health, wealth, and power by being prepared, perceptive, and adaptable. Creatively manifest your will with wisdom, compassion, and vigilance. Be wary of the onset of ennui. Enjoy the adventure.

1 ✦ THE WIZARD

Essence
Produce effects through knowledge and willpower.

Question
Do I align my will and actions with the principles of nature or do I lack willpower and act incompetent? Have I sought to understand the elements of power and threads of continuity within the arts and sciences?

Revelation
The Wizard card symbolizes the effectiveness of knowledge and willpower. According to legend, a Wizard took the time to become educated about forms of magic in order to cast spells (manipulation of reality through education). Comprehension and determination enable the handling of affairs. Ignorance and indecision lead to failure.

An understanding of the arts and sciences will provide the framework for an informed point of view and actionable intelligence; increasing the probability of successfully achieving goals. Each area of study at a university represents knowledge worthy of consideration; but do not limit study to defined curriculums. Learn the limits of current knowledge to help mankind progress. Apply a unique mix of experience, intelligence, and will towards discovering something new. Seek the points at which the frontiers of the arts and sciences intersect with business to tap into practical cutting-edge applications for generating wealth.

Make a map of interests and pathways to achievement. Do the research and develop the willpower to make something happen, to produce an effect, to cast a spell.

2 ✦ THE PRIESTESS

Essence
Use intuition to help make good decisions.

Question
Do I process knowledge subconsciously so that I may perceive an intuitive idea or do I ignore my gut feelings and instincts and decline to develop keen intuition?

Revelation
The High Priestess card symbolizes the power of intuition to guide action through insight. Intuition was a powerful and mysterious form of wisdom revered by the ancients—often accessed through rhythmic movement and deep reflection. By developing the power of your intuition, you will have a useful tool in any situation that requires a decision.

An informed point of view enables intuition much more than a shallow, superficial level of knowledge. When contemplating a matter of interest or a problem, obtain adequate experience and relevant knowledge to enable the subconscious mind to process and organize the information at its own pace. Your subconscious will reveal insights to the conscious mind later, if properly prepared. The mind processes and organizes data while sleeping, dreaming, meditating, exercising, and relaxing in trance states—leading to intuitive insight and heightened perceptions. Predictive intuition occurs in the prepared mind when confronted with changing circumstances. This applies both physically and mentally. The elements, combinations, and various movements are practiced so often that tapping them at the right time in a given situation becomes a natural reaction. Immerse yourself in all of the available data about your interest and develop a sense for the right move.

The more in depth your knowledge as discussed in the Wizard symbol, the more likely you will be correct when making a decision based on a hunch as advised by the Priestess symbol.

3 ✦ THE EMPRESS

Essence
Create what you need.

Question
Do I put into effect my creativity by understanding and stimulating the creative process? Or, do I lack creativity due to my own poverty of experience? Am I unable to manifest my will because of a lack of knowledge and intuition? What skills do I need to acquire in my area of interest to enable a level of mastery that will facilitate innovation?

Revelation
The symbol of the Empress represents the power wielded by those who are creative and productive. Fertility cult rituals for the reproduction of plants, animals, and people revolve around the theme of successfully combining elements to facilitate the emergence of new life, whether it is a bountiful harvest or a healthy newborn. Wasteful dissipation of resources makes creation very difficult.

Creativity is the act of manifesting that which is envisioned in the mind. Skills, knowledge, resources, and willpower are the essential ingredients. Knowledge of relevant patterns occurs with immersion in a topic. Applied effort is needed to develop talents and gather resources. The willpower to start implementing ideas distinguishes the creative and productive.

The Empress encourages the channeling of the immense power of creativity. Explore and map the frontiers of knowledge in the area that you wish to transform. Apply your unique perspective to create useful and interesting innovations.

4 ✦ THE EMPEROR

Essence
Take advantage of opportunities through leadership.

Question
Can I envision and achieve a goal by developing and implementing a sound strategy? Have I attained the vision and skills necessary to lead both myself and others?

Revelation
The card of the Emperor represents leadership. An Emperor has traditionally been vested with the power to lead people to victory. Ineffectiveness and confusion render an Emperor dangerous. Initiative and adaptability encourage supporters and facilitate success.

An Emperor must understand strategy, operations, and tactics in order to envision alternative ways to accomplish goals. A strategy is a broad operating framework for achieving a goal. Operations consist of the missions that are taken to implement a specific strategy. Tactics include the various ways that you can conduct your missions. Build a competent team to lead to victory while simultaneously expanding personal capabilities. Take a genuine interest in the skills, experience, and goals of others, to bring out their full potential and inspire them to win. Encourage your team by giving them autonomy to innovate within parameters that facilitate tactical adaptations. Learn to recognize whether a strategy is succeeding or not and be flexible enough to replace a failed strategy so that your team can innovate within a winning framework.

Envisioning possibilities, acquiring skills, building a team, equipping with the proper gear, and conducting meaningful action to produce victory are the duty and privilege of a leader. Have a plan, know yourself and your team, and make it happen.

5 ✦ THE HIGH PRIEST/ MONK/HEIROPHANT

Essence
Develop habits that will lead to success.

Question
Do I practice effective habits that facilitate mental, physical, and spiritual development? Or, am I ignorant of beneficial rituals? Am I too lazy to develop useful habits?

Revelation
The Hierophant represents the power of rituals and habits. Priests, monks, druids, shamans and other spiritual leaders have always been regarded as conduits of power in numerous belief systems. Rituals such as meditation, prayer, fasting, and exercise are faithfully performed to attain enlightenment and power.

Performing useful habits will develop talents and facilitate the accomplishment of goals. Alternatively, bad habits such as overindulgence and neglectfulness are akin to being utterly faithless towards progress and generally lead to ruin. An informed point of view will enable useful activity in areas of likely growth and opportunity. Develop a comprehensive perspective to determine success factors. Applied efforts toward mastering a domain ensure learning.

Guided by the faith that good habits are keys to success, use willpower and devotion to ingrain useful behaviors until they become second nature. Regularly seek activities that develop strength, agility, health, intellect, good judgment, and charisma. Achieve a fluid level of mastery to vastly increase the probability of victory. Thrive in your adventures as a reward for faithful devotion to progress.

6 ✦ THE LOVERS

Essence
Develop symbiotic relationships.

Question
Am I attracted to the people and situations that enable growth, strength, and pleasure or am I caught in a pattern that stifles development, fosters weakness or malevolence, and causes distress?

Revelation
The Lovers card symbolizes the development of relationships and the effect they have on those involved. The Lovers symbol calls for reflection and action regarding relationships.

People develop mutual interests. The ideal relationship is mutually beneficial—whether considering relationships between husband and wife, boyfriend and girlfriend, friends, family, business contacts, communities of interests, nations, countries, or species. Positively, individuals in groups can strengthen and aid each other while attaining goals and enjoying life together. Interactions among groups of people lead to skill development, knowledge, and actionable intelligence. Teamwork and cooperation foster victory. Win/win techniques for producing relationships and deals that benefit all parties should be studied, developed and practiced.

Sometimes associations are unreliable and negative; draining time and energy. Bad associations can lead to misery, bankruptcy, and war. At other times malevolent groups may infuse each other with energy for destructive ends such as the stifling of reasonable thought, incitement of violence against the innocent, or a mutually reinforcing path of frenzied hostile behavior. Change the dynamic of unfriendly relations from exploitative and negative to helpful, if possible.

People and situations that are somehow aligned with your beliefs and predominant thoughts may be attracted to you. Associate with various communities that are enthusiastic about interests that attract you while simultaneously keeping an open mind to discovering new interests.

Whether instructing or listening, knowledge is often enhanced and organized through sharing. Experience other cultures to attain new and interesting perspectives, wisdom, and friends.

If you ensure that the relationships you develop are symbiotic, then your network of allies will grow. By showing a genuine interest in others and their activities, people will be inclined to befriend you. The emphasis is on "genuine", as each person has a unique story to tell and interests worth considering. Avoid relationships that are not win/win.

7 ✦ THE CHARIOT

Essence
Establish control and time your actions to achieve victory.

Question
Am I able to balance and channel the turbulent force of emotions? Can I transform knowledge into effective action that, with proper timing enables me to overcome challenges? Do I lack control of the powerful sources of inspiration, direction, and timing, leaving me helplessly hurtling forward through time?

Revelation
The Chariot card symbolizes the ability to influence forces with consummate timing to achieve a victory. Charioteers controlled powerful animals to drive their chariot for sport or combat. A charioteer used reins to control the horses, wheels to enable efficient movement, and a platform from which to position and skillfully deploy weaponry.

The use of tools coupled with timing is equivalent to a charioteer controlling his chariot and horses in a manner that will lead to victory. Additionally, control over emotions is akin to control over the turbulent power of animals that pull the chariot. Maneuver with the rhythm of the circumstance whether aligning cooperatively with a team or breaking the pattern of an enemy.

Control of your emotions enables you to focus energy derived from passionate feelings towards a purpose. Generate excitement before initiating activity and focus the energy towards your goals. Emotions, if uncontrolled by you will control you, like a chariot without reins. Utter decadence regarding maintenance and control will lead to disaster. Banish procrastination and initiate useful action.

Controlling emotions, deploying useful tools, and developing a keen sense of timing will aid advancement towards victory.

8 ✦ JUSTICE

Essence
Understand cause and effect over time.

Question
Do I recognize the justice of nature—cause and effect—in that what I do now will effect both the present and future? Do I prepare via relevant training? Do I engage in a sound manner? Do I procrastinate to the point of being unprepared or unsuccessful?

Revelation
The sort of Justice that this card symbolizes is nature's justice. By recognizing the natural justice of cause and effect, you can predictably increase or decrease your health and wealth over time. All habits—both good and bad—will produce results.

Identify the effect you desire to produce, determine the causes of making it happen, and just do it. Continuous improvement and useful action will lead to rewards and success. Accordingly, a bias will lead to poor judgment and useless work. A complete lack of trying will always yield failure. This is fair and impartial justice at work as it applies to everyone and all matters.

If you follow the guidance of the Tarot Symbols of the Major Arcana, you will greatly increase the odds of achieving your goal as determined by Justice. By seeking out and using proven methodologies for success, you are combining the navigation of the Star with the habits of the Monk guided by knowledge of the Wizard in a way that recognizes the presence of Justice.

9 ✦ THE HERMIT

Essence
Develop insight.

Question
Do I periodically withdraw from my daily routines to assess my current lifestyle and modus operandi? Have I neglected to take the time to reflect and study my situation out of ignorance, laziness, fear, or procrastination? Where can I contemplate my inner and outer lives –what I am doing, what I have done, what I would like to do, what I believe and how I think?

Revelation
The Hermit symbolizes the wisdom that can be gained by withdrawing from your day to day activities and focusing on your situation. Hermits are traditionally viewed as people who leave society to contemplate affairs and develop profound wisdom. Often, they have been sought out for advice on a course of action due to their acute perceptions regarding thought, feeling, behavior, and situations. Wise counsel is not sought from those who live the folly of never bothering to learn lessons, reflect, or grow. Stimulate actionable insight by getting away from routine to reflect and contemplate matters.

By removing ourselves from familiar situations, we are forced to think. Different cultures and geographical environments will stimulate thinking. Travel, observe, and interact. Notice similarities and differences. By interacting in various environments, many types of fitness are developed. Gaming is another way to stimulate thinking by playing with models that simulate aspects of life. By conducting a critical evaluation of ourselves, others, and our environment, we will be better able to align behavior and resources with goals.

The interplay between The Hermit and The Priest is symbiotic. They each provide relief from and inform the other and can even be thought of as part of the same—analyzing and practicing. Meditation, contemplation, reflection, and visualization will facilitate useful action. By taking a bit of time every day to reflect on matters and a lengthier period away from routine periodically, efficient and determined action will be stimulated—whether that is towards an enhanced performance of current activities or a complete course correction.

10 ✦ THE WHEEL OF FORTUNE

Essence
Adapt to changes in the environment.

Question
Do I recognize that my environment is constantly changing and attempt to adapt via skill development and mastery of timing or do I obstinately resist recognizing patterns and simply fail to course correct because of ignorance, sluggishness, unpreparedness, or despair?

Revelation
The Wheel of Fortune represents changing circumstances and your ability to adapt. Dealing successfully with change requires keen perception and useful skills. Mankind has survived because it has successfully adapted to changing weather patterns, animal behavior, and plant growth cycles.

Survivors recognize the patterns of nature and make use of resources skillfully. The alternative to successful adaptation is misfortune—culminating in impoverished death. Fortune changes, so be prepared. Unforeseen events happen with regularity. Recognize and address the situation at hand. Know your environment, develop the skills and systems needed to thrive, build the team to win, and acquire the gear to succeed.

Develop sound perspective and able skill by educating yourself as described under the Wizard symbol, train as noted in the Monk, and maintain awareness as epitomized by the symbol of the Moon so that you can react successfully to the vagaries of The Wheel of Fortune. Be able to react to changes beyond your control through continuous learning, innovation, skill development, and a good sense of awareness.

11 ✦ STRENGTH/LUST

Essence
Use passions as sources of energy, drive, and power.

Question
Do I derive power from my desires, cultivate passionate vitality, and apply this enthusiastic energy towards my goals? Am I overcome with fear, sloth, or failure of will to the point where I am too weak to achieve my ambitions?

Revelation
Strength is the core ingredient of all accomplishments. You get your strength from your passion for activity—your will to work, play, and thrive. That's why this symbol is sometimes called Strength and sometimes called Lust.

Exulting in dynamic action is a source of great power. Those who neither seek interests nor curiously and enthusiastically pursue activities are generally cursed with weakness, depression, ennui, and a sense of malaise. Competition and cooperation, training and experience, are proven ways to develop strength, if done in a motivated way. A leader will build win/win relationships to tap the passion and strength of a team. The ability to thrive despite adversity is evidence of core strength.

Identify something that you are keenly interested in exploring and determine what strengths are needed for success. Imagine the rewards of vigorous effort. Get fired up and have your faculties fully engaged when you begin.

12 ✦ THE HANGED MAN

Essence
Attain enlightenment regarding needed metamorphosis.

Question
Am I enlightened enough to recognize what is inhibiting my plans and facilitating my ruin or am I hung up and deceived by my own distorted thinking, tunnel vision, and limiting beliefs?

Revelation
The Hanged Man symbolizes a person at the crossroads of self discovery, suspended from action. Some cultures engage in rituals that involve some sort of ordeal in order to transform into a more powerful and wise being. Perhaps this sort of shock therapy is a powerful way for people to face their errors and course correct, or recognize their challenges and adjust course. The Hanged Man can use this time for insightful contemplation, enlightenment, and beneficial metamorphosis or fruitless complaint. It flows naturally into the Death card because the person must choose whether to emerge as a different being or stagnate due to inertia.

Take the opportunity to identify a problem that is preventing your success. By acknowledging problems, you will have the opportunity to eliminate them. Recognize your weaknesses, false beliefs, bad decisions, poor habits, unsound perceptions, unhelpful acquaintances, and goals not aligned with your desires for they are the facilitators of your ruin and will confound you consistently.

Enjoy the increased capacity for power that comes with enlightenment and the process of transforming into a more powerful being as you learn from your ordeals.

13 ✦ DEATH

Essence
Solve problems, eliminate inaccurate perceptions, and end bad habits.

Question
Have I eliminated things that inhibit my plans or facilitate my ruin or am I trapped by my own inertia, stagnation, or addiction by refusing to end something detrimental? Have I ended something that I should not have ended?

Revelation
The Death card symbolizes the end of something—preferably a problem as opposed to something useful. Ideally, experience the death of bad habits, bad perceptions, bad associates, and worthless goals in order to close or finish a malignant way of being. Be wary of ending something of value. Evolve/transcend/actualize towards adaptability and enlightenment,

Recognize problems and solve them. Replace bad habits with good ones. Lethargy and laziness can keep one mired in a stagnant way of life. Inaction spawned by indolence is a contributor to loss. If a strategy is flawed or tactic is failing, cease, desist, and develop a new way to attain your goal. A leader must build and maintain a winning team by adding and releasing players based upon the needed skills for the task; or upgrading the player's capabilities.

The intelligence that you have personally developed via your numerous experiences should be acted upon in a way that eliminates unhealthy habits while maintaining positive adaptations. Seek activity that leads to health, wealth, adventure, worthiness, fun, and victory while ending detrimental activities.

The ending of one thing usually means more time for another, so replace something self destructive with something enriching and positive.

14 ✦ TEMPERANCE/ART

Essence
Create useful tools and manage resources.

Question
Have I managed resources effectively in order to create something useful? Do I know the elemental parts of tools? Have I been wasteful and failed to create a needed tool because of a lack of knowledge, a lack of preparation, or a lack of self-control?

Revelation
The Art or Temperance card represents combining your resources to create useful tools. A mind capable of advanced tool creation is the competitive advantage of humans (language, pictures, symbols, concepts, writing, wheels, plows, computers, guns, etc.). If united elements are unsuitable or lacking, you may end up with something that could become explosive or poisonous or useless. Join resources in harmonious and thrifty ways to create valuable tools and concepts.

All combinations can either lead to success or ruin based upon the care and skill of the creator. An artist mixes colors and materials to make art that enhances the viewer's perspective. A blacksmith merges metals, fire, and water to produce weapons, armor, and farming tools. Soldiers must create sound strategies, conduct relevant missions to complete operations, and use adaptive combined arms tactics to ensure mission success—all based on varying environmental conditions and different opponents. A businessman combines raw materials, human resources, and capital to create and sell a product in response to a shifting market using the concept of a business plan. An athlete refines drills, practice, and cross training in order to play at maximum capability within a distinct field. A chemist can combine elements that are productive or deadly. Scientists and engineers combine forms of matter to create medicine and industrial components.

After you determine your goals, you will discover what elements you need to acquire, learn how to harvest and combine them, and create the things you need.

15 ✦ THE DEVIL

Essence
Balance temptation and concentration to enable both exploration and achievement.

Question
Are my desires aligned with my goals or are they leading me towards ruin? Do I have the ability to control and understand my behavior? Am I aware of my environment? When I start an activity, am I unable to finish it due to constant distractions or do I focus on it so single-mindedly that I cease to explore? Am I able to make things happen without incurring detrimental consequences?

Revelation
The Devil represents the temptation and distraction that can lead to ruin. The mind is restless and constantly curious. While curiosity is an excellent stimulus to exploration, develop the self discipline to complete important activities. Evil influences and destructive experiences can lead to utter disaster. Concentration and self-discipline are necessary to resist temptations and achieve goals.

Focus on your plan and accomplish your objectives. Increase strength, passion, concentration, and exploration by aligning your desires with your goals. Balance curiosity and focus in a way that enables both discovery and accomplishment. Adapting to unforeseen events, researching innovations, and investigating opportunities are to be distinguished from useless and malevolent distractions. Be disciplined enough to break unhelpful addictions. Be aware enough to take advantage of opportunities.

As you become healthier, wealthier, and more powerful don't become complacent, lazy, distracted, and inattentive. Identify temptations and bad habits that lure you away from your goals as noted in the Hanged Man. Resist temptation and concentrate on your work lest you fail to achieve as warned by the Devil symbol. Develop your interests while also conducting the activities necessary to maintain and accrue power.

16 ✦ THE TOWER

Essence
Build strengths, consolidate gains, and progress to new frontiers.

Power Question
Do I have a strong base of skills from which to adventure? Do I have a viewpoint about an area in which to progress? Am I trapped in a confining way of life due to a lack of insight or ability?

Revelation
The Tower symbolizes the strategic imperative to build upon your strengths and to expand further; as opposed to hiding behind your past glories with the illusion of security. In the past, castles were used to secure land and provide a base for further expansion. Lords that used the castles as a base to project power and influence were generally not taken by surprise. Some lords hid away in their castles and only looked as far as their small domain. They were generally conquered by other lords with expansionist tendencies.

Dwelling in an oppressive rut can lead to catastrophic failure. Utilize the knowledge and strength that you currently have as a base for expansion rather than a fortress in which to hide. Build outwards from your current base of familiarity and power. You must be vigilant and build on your past successes, rather than being imprisoned with a lack of insight or a lack of will due to complacency.

Using strengths to progress is essential to continued survival. A nation must know the art of war, maintain both economic and technological advantages, and cultivate both loyal citizens and allies in order to protect its interests in a sustainable fashion. A nation that fosters a culture of freedom, self-reliance coupled with teamwork, and martial vigor tempered with compassion will find that it expands its influence in a positive way. Major wars can be avoided and economies can be built by becoming actively engaged in foreign lands in a mutually beneficial way. Coaches and traders and businessmen must not rest on one winning plan or training regimen because others are sure to copy the plan or adapt or exploit. Students must continue to learn beyond school. As it is with groups of ten, hundreds, or millions, so it is with the individual.

Explore new environments and develop new capabilities as a matter of course. Take note of communities of interest such as the political, business, environmental, intellectual, artistic, musical, athletic, cultural, and martial communities in as many lands as possible. Not only be open minded to new ideas, but actively seek to expand the domains of your awareness and capabilities. Use your strength to progress further.

17 ✦ THE STAR

Essence
Use guides to navigate and course correct when necessary.

Power Question
Do I seek guidance and understanding that can help me find my way towards my goals or do I ignore opportunities for enlightenment and learning?

Revelation
The Star card symbolizes the usefulness of navigational aids. Sailors once used the stars to navigate the oceans. Ancients used the stars to mark the cyclical passage of time which led to the development of the calendar. Those unwilling or unable to seek useful information, advice, or guidance are often unsuccessful in their endeavors as they become lost along the way due to lack of preparation. Use the resources around you to navigate your own field of challenge.

The competitive advantage of humanity lies in the ability to transmit information symbolically so that the accumulated wisdom of ages can be accessed and built upon—the supreme tools of language and writing. Build upon the knowledge of generations rather than relying only upon your instincts. By seeking out signs, symbols, leaders, the knowledgeable, media, books, gear, and maps of various fields of endeavor, you can efficiently and effectively master a domain. You may be the next to manifest an innovation that others use to help themselves traverse a domain.

Knowing how, where, and when to take action will save you time and ensure success. Learn from the example of successful people and organizations. Enjoy your explorations by being prepared, aware, adaptable, and creative. Seek leading indicators that foreshadow patterns. Metaphorically and literally, know how to read a map to help ensure that you thrive in your adventures.

18 ✢ THE MOON

Essence
Develop accurate perceptions.

Question
Am I aware of the cycles within nature that encompass both behavior and events? Do I understand the forms of darkness that lurk within people such as deception, violence, fascination, and superstition? Do I channel the power of dreams, visions, passions, symbols, and various lenses of perception? Do I refuse to deal with reality by escaping into daydreams, prejudice, superstition, fear and lunacy?

Revelation
The Moon symbolizes the cyclical nature of events and varying degrees of perception ranging from lunacy to lucidity. As the Moon controls the ebb and flow of the oceans and is visually cyclical, it represents the constant shifting that occurs in all matters for many occultists. Occultists of many eras believe that this world is but a reflection or extension of another spiritual world. Occultists often try to control or influence the people and events of this world, by channeling the influence of the spiritual world.

Knowing how to actually make things happen in this world distinguishes the lucid from the lunatic. Perception is a personal experience—a filtering of reality through the senses and the mind. Everyone perceives people, places, and events a bit differently. Being able to perceive accurately is a key to success in all endeavors.

Alter your perceptions in various ways to attain a broader view and explore your senses in a way that yields insight. Gather intelligence to form an insightful perspective of the environment and of the competition. Plants and animals continuously engage in deception and camouflage in order to compete successfully in nature. Competitors in all fields of endeavor use deception and surprise to achieve victory. Soldiers, businessmen, poker players, traders, and athletes all use deception and surprise to attain victory and profit. Players will act in ways to confuse and mislead competitors. The various players in any system will each have a unique perspective that is often right and occasionally wrong to varying degrees. Be able to determine patterns, trends, and rhythms.

If you intend to be consistently successful, accurate perception (lucidity), as opposed to poor perceptions based on irrational conclusions (lunacy) is necessary. Be wary.

19 ✦ THE SUN

Essence
Absorb energy for renewal, clarity, and growth.

Question
Do the systems that I have developed give energy, regeneration, clarity, and pleasure or do my systems sap inspiration and cause disharmony, failure, delusion, and misery?

Revelation:
The Sun represents energy, regeneration, clarity, and life. If the Sun were to burn out, the world would be shrouded in darkness and life would end. If goals are unclear and effort seems like drudgery, then an influx of power as symbolized by the Sun is necessary to progress.

Energy is essential for accomplishment and can be channeled to create the life of your choice. The more ambitious your choices, the more energy you will need to channel. Utilize the rich depth of nature, the collective excitation of groups, the sights of beauty, the sounds of music, and the diversity of cities to absorb energy. Eat healthy food, drink lots of water, and exercise thoroughly to facilitate a mind that thinks clearly and a body teeming with vigor. Discover personal motivations and use them to generate drive.

In order to develop plans with confidence and pursue opportunities with vigor, people need a source of positive motivation and clear goals. By constant renewal of enthusiasm you can lead yourself and others towards achievement. The Sun rejuvenates and clarifies the ambitions of The Emperor and stimulates Strength/Lust; enabling peak performance.

20 ✦ JUDGMENT/AEON/ THE ANGEL

Essence
Take necessary risks, engage in action, and judge progress.

Question
Am I enjoying the results of my accomplishments or have I refused to make decisions, failed to take action, and declined to evaluate the outcomes of my endeavors?

Revelation
This card is sometimes called Judgment and at other times called the Angel or Aeon. This card is symbolic of the angels at the end of an era (eon) rendering judgment on your role in shaping events. Be a judge of your own behavior and situation. Determine areas for improvement and progress. Analyzing the positive and negative feedback that you receive from deeds will provide the intelligence for adaptations to your environment.

Engage different environments in order to develop resilient fitness. Adapt by making sound judgments. Conduct a sincere appraisal of yourself and your team in order to improve performance. Make decisions, take risks, and conduct the necessary activities to achieve goals.

Perceptions shrouded by falsehood or denial coupled with a refusal to evaluate lead to failure. Weakness, disillusionment, or procrastination can result in failure. Needed action must be taken in a timely manner.

If you do not progress via useful action as counseled by Judgment/Aeon/ The Angel, you will not master The World for you will be unable to conduct a grand synthesis of your experiences and knowledge. It would be difficult to conduct a synthesis of your lessons learned if you did not venture forth and give your ideas a try. Go forth and create the world you desire.

21 ✦ THE WORLD

Essence
Develop wisdom and strength from experience.

Question
Have I gained control of my environment and myself to the point that I enjoy the adventures of the world with all the accompanying growth, learning, and pleasure or have I failed to comprehend the principles of energy, synthesize the realms of knowledge, and develop the capacity for happiness due to a poverty of experience?

Revelation
The World card symbolizes experiences and opportunities in the world. While the World card does come at the end of the deck, the Tarot system requires regular consideration of the symbols in both a linear and nonlinear fashion. This systematic comparison of progress and actions towards goals enables success in the World, develops wisdom, and fosters strength. Conduct analysis, whether victorious or defeated, to prepare for the next challenge.

If you have lived the positive aspects of the cards, then you will most likely be reflecting on your victories and progress. The will to win coupled with intelligent action generally leads to victory, a true cause for hope no matter your circumstance. As you actualize your goals and conceive new possibilities, you realize that the whole world lies before you to explore and adventure within.

If you have lived the negative aspects of the cards, you will most likely be ruefully considering your stagnation and failures. Even worse, you may not be considering your problems at all, but merely festering in the bitter fruit of stagnant rot. Whether it's due to blind oblivion or obstinate neglect, unsolved problems remain troublesome and even ruinous. Dwell in squalor or progress; you get to choose.

Having reference points for much that you encounter enables a certain richness and depth of perception, to go along with the sense of wonderment and adventure when doing something new. Synthesize experiences with knowledge of history, current events, and future projections. Notice how many fields of endeavor share similar attributes for both success and failure.

By maintaining and upgrading your level of awareness, adaptability, and creativity, you will be prepared and enjoy life's adventures and challenges. A rich base of knowledge and experience, coupled with wisdom and willpower, will lead to health, wealth, and power. While threads of continuity exist in the world—such as the winning principles of the Tarot—the environment is always changing—stimulating your continued metamorphosis towards success. With luck and effort, you can enjoy the World!

Symbols in Linear Flow as Positive Advice

0 **The Fool:** Impulse leads to action.
1 **The Wizard:** Use knowledge and willpower to produce effects.
2 **The Priestess:** Use intuition to help make good decisions.
3 **The Empress:** Create what you need.
4 **The Emperor:** Take advantage of opportunities through leadership.
5 **The Priest/Monk/Hierophant:** Develop habits that lead to success.
6 **The Lovers:** Develop symbiotic relationships.
7 **The Chariot:** Establish control and time your actions to achieve victory.
8 **Justice:** Understand cause and effect over time.
9 **The Hermit:** Develop insight.
10 **The Wheel of Fortune:** Adapt to changes in the environment.
11 **Strength/Lust:** Use passions as sources of energy, drive, and power.
12 **The Hanged Man:** Attain enlightenment regarding needed metamorphosis.
13 **Death:** Solve problems, eliminate inaccurate perceptions, and end bad habits.
14 **Temperance/Art:** Create useful tools and manage resources.
15 **The Devil:** Balance temptation/concentration to successfully explore/achieve.
16 **The Tower:** Build strengths, consolidate gains, and progress to new frontiers.
17 **The Star:** Use guides to navigate and course correct when necessary.
18 **The Moon:** Develop accurate perceptions.
19 **The Sun:** Absorb energy for renewal, clarity, and growth.
20 **Judgment/Aeon/Angel:** Take necessary risks, engage in action, and judge progress.
21 **The World:** Develop wisdom and strength from experience.
0 **The Fool:** Your next impulse . . .

Three Examples of Nonlinear Positive Flow Interpretations

Passion is the energy source (Strength) for habits (Priest), which should ideally be leading towards the goal (Emperor) thought of originally as just an idea (Fool). Using reason and knowledge (Wizard), guided by intuition (Priestess), begin to create (Empress) the world envisioned. While developing and implementing a plan by leading (Emperor) a team (Lovers) to achieve the goal, take time to reflect on the lessons learned (Hermit) and course correct if necessary (Wheel of Fortune). By recognizing (The Hanged Man) and eliminating (Death) obstacles to your progress whether they are bad habits, bad associates or poor perceptions, successfully traverse between temptation and concentration (The Devil). By precise control (Chariot), productive resource utilization (Temperance/Art), and good habits (Priest) over time (Justice), awareness and adaptability towards changing circumstances (Wheel of Fortune) while moving towards the goal (Fool), occur naturally. By methodically building upon past success (Tower) and seeking new and useful areas to explore and learn (Star), develop a keen perception of the environment and people (Moon). By constant renewal and regeneration via healthy living (Sun), maintain the clarity and energy (Sun) to take the necessary risks and engage in profitable action (Judgment). Victories will provide the joy for living and the knowledge for further adventure (The World). Experience another impulse that forms a goal (The Fool)...

Summoning energy (Sun) and channeling it towards desires (Strength/Lust) do the rituals to prepare (Priest/Monk/Hierophant) for more adventures (Fool). (Justice) will determine whether future efforts will succeed. As (Emperor), conquer new territory (Tower). The (Wizard) and (Priestess) render advice based on intuition developed from knowledge. The (Hermit) reflects upon the timing and effectiveness of moves towards victory (Chariot). The (Empress) will help to create useful tools (Temperance/Art). Guided by the (Star) and adapting to changes (Wheel of Fortune), avoid distraction while exploring ideas (The Devil). Eliminate (Death) the problematic (Hanged Man) and cultivate allies (Lovers). Your keen perception (Moon) enables successful risk taking and achievement (Aeon/Judgment). Enjoy and learn from your experiences (World).

Impulsively, decide to manifest an idea. Use reason and intuition towards productive creativity. Self control, teamwork, and applied effort enable accomplishment over time and foster wisdom. Changes in fortune are exciting opportunities for growth. Decisive action makes way for creative solutions to goals. Advancing forward, navigate cycles with keen perception. Energetically conduct bold action for success.

An Example of Nonlinear Negative Flow

Lack of passion renders a fatigue so debilitating that it leaves one too tired and too unmotivated to engage in useful habits—leaving goals unfulfilled and ideas undeveloped. Unwilling to explore areas of interest, uninformed intuition fails to lead to useful creative ideas. Drifting without a plan, actions are aimless and reflections are absent. Opportunities are lost completely or unexploited. Luck always seems bad because failing to see opportunities during changing circumstances leads to problems. Failing to recognize problems with the approach and not bothering to eliminate harmful influences, confounded efforts abound and progress is consistently stifled. Constantly tempted by impulsive desires, lacking the ability to concentrate for very long on things that are important, self control is absent and resources are wasted. Over time, poor habits result in ignorance and weakness. Trapped in a rut, stagnation and lack of exploration have led to poor perceptions, the company of lunatics, and vicious cycles of ruin. Unclear and unenthused about taking risks or engaging in activity, little of merit is accomplished. Failing at most things and mired in misery, lack of knowledge is demoralizing. Another impulse forms that will be recklessly or fleetingly followed, if at all…

If this paragraph resonates with you, then here's some good news in one respect. You've identified what's holding you back and you now have 21 steps to guide in course correction. This book will empower you to recognize a situation and deal with it per your will.

Acknowledgements

The distillation of the wisdom contained in the symbols of the Tarot and relayed in this book is the direct result of my interaction with people, places, and useful things coupled with the desire to produce an item of utility for those seeking to improve their situation. I thank much and wish well to all who contribute to our collective well being.

A special thanks to Rosana Jakob, the artist who created the images for the Major Arcana interpretation found in this book. She presently designs and inks customized tattoos, based out of her lovely shop in Amsterdam. She can be reached at www.myspace.com/dermadonna if you are interested in experiencing artwork on your skin at the hands of a talented tattoo artist.

A final thanks goes to all those who read, write, or teach others to do so. Herein lays the manifestation of the competitive advantage of the human race: symbolic thought.

www.ingramcontent.com/pod-product-compliance
Lightning Source LLC
Chambersburg PA
CBHW042333150426
43194CB00001B/46